FOOD WEBS

GRASSLAND

Food Webs

By William Anthony

KidHaven
PUBLISHING

Published in 2021 by
KidHaven Publishing, an Imprint of Greenhaven Publishing, LLC
353 3rd Avenue
Suite 255
New York, NY 10010

Edited by: Madeline Tyler
Designed by: Jasmine Pointer

Find us on

Cataloging-in-Publication Data

Names: Anthony, William.
Title: Grassland food webs / William Anthony.
Description: New York : KidHaven Publishing, 2021. | Series: Food webs | Includes glossary and index.
Identifiers: ISBN 9781534535206 (pbk.) | ISBN 9781534535220 (library bound) | ISBN 9781534535213 (6 pack) | ISBN 9781534535237 (ebook)
Subjects: LCSH: Grassland ecology--Juvenile literature. | Grassland plants--Juvenile literature. | Grassland animals--Juvenile literature. | Food chains (Ecology)--Juvenile literature.
Classification: LCC QH541.5.P7 A584 2021 | DDC 577.4--dc23

Printed in the United States of America

CPSIA compliance information: Batch #BS20K: For further information contact Greenhaven Publishing LLC, New York, New York at 1-844-317-7404.

Please visit our website, www.greenhavenpublishing.com. For a free color catalog of all our high-quality books, call toll free 1-844-317-7404 or fax 1-844-317-7405.

Photo credits:
Images are courtesy of Shutterstock.com with thanks to Getty Images, Thinkstock Photo, and iStockphoto.

aradaphotography (earth texture), YamabikaY (paper texture). Front cover - Ian Rentoul, Patthana Nirangkul, Kanea, Leo Blanchette. 2 – Volodymyr Burdiak. 3 – nuruddean. 4&5 – JaySi. 6 – Edmund O'Connor, Black Sheep Media, Dirk M. de Boer. 7 – markusmayer, Benny Marty, PHOTOCREO Michal Bednarek. 6 & 7 – aodaodaodaod. 8 – SAROJ GURJAR. 9 – EcoPrint, ArCaLu, John Michael Vosloo, Eric Isselee. 10 – Stuart G Porter. 11 – Svetography, Stacey Ann Alberts, NaturesMomentsuk, Bob Pool. 12 – Beate Wolter, Edmund O'Connor, Black Sheep Media. 13 – Eric Isselee, Dr Ajay Kumar Singh, Pavel Krasensky. 14 – EcoPrint. 15 – Ana Gram, Edwin Godinho, Succulent, nwdph. 16 – Carlos A Antunes, Simon Eeman. 17 – Simon Eeman, Johan Swanepoel. 18 – Ondrej Prosicky. 19 – Eric Isselee, Stuart G Porter, Nicola Destefano. 20 – PACO COMO. 21 – Eric Isselee, E X P L O R E R. 23 – Thomas Retterath.

CONTENTS

Words that look like THIS can be found in the glossary on page 24.

IN THE GRASSLANDS

Go on a safari, see the wonderful sights... but be careful! Do you know who might be sneaking through the tall grass, looking for a meal?

There are lots of different animals and plants to be found, all going about their daily business, and each and every one of them has a place in the food web.

Let's look at who eats who in the grasslands. Who can we find in the African SAVANNA...?

THE FOOD WEB

...HERBIVORES eat the plants...

It all starts with the sun's energy...

...which feeds plants...

...CARNIVORES eat the herbivores...

...and APEX PREDATORS eat those.

...bigger PREDATORS eat them...

7

THE LION

Keep your distance—I'm a lion, and I'm an apex predator here in the African savanna. That means I never have to look out for someone wanting to eat me because I'm too big and strong! It also means I have lots of PREY to choose from for my dinner...

NAME:	Lion
TYPE:	MAMMAL
HOME:	Africa
FOOD:	Carnivore
PREDATOR OR PREY?:	Apex Predator

Hare: small but a great snack...?

Wildebeest: strong but a big feast...?

Thomson's gazelle: quick but delicious...?

I'm bored of eating the same old things. I want a special treat. What's that over there in the grass? It looks tasty...

QUICK, TURN THE PAGE!

THE CARACAL

I'm a caracal, and I really don't want to mess with that lion. We are both a type of cat, but lions are one of the biggest cats in the world! If I can stay out of sight, I can get on with finding my own food.

NAME:	Caracal
TYPE:	Mammal
HOME:	Africa and Asia
FOOD:	Carnivore
PREDATOR OR PREY?:	Both

Mongoose: furry but definitely not friendly...?

Hare: jumpy but juicy...?

Thomson's gazelle: big but delicious...?

All that worry about the lion has made me lose my appetite. Well, maybe I could just have a small snack instead...

WHO'S THE SNACK?

THE MOUSE

I may be snack-sized for all the animals that want to eat me, but that also means I'm harder for them to spot! Besides, I have to worry about a different type of animal when it comes to food...

NAME:	Mouse
TYPE:	Mammal
HOME:	All Over the World
FOOD:	Herbivore
PREDATOR OR PREY?:	Prey

I have to compete with the other herbivores for my food. I love eating different types of grass, but so do these animals:

Hare: a furry issue...

Harvester ant: a nippy nuisance...

Topi: a horned problem...

IS **THAT A HARE?**

THE HARE

Herbivores all have to share. We can't afford to spend time fighting over food while there are lots of predators on our tails! I'm a hare, and I have a lot of big animals after me for their dinner...

NAME:	Hare
TYPE:	Mammal
HOME:	Africa, North America, Europe, and Asia
FOOD:	Herbivore
PREDATOR OR PREY?:	Prey

All of these animals see me as a tasty treat, but I don't plan on being on their menus any time soon.

Lion: scary teeth...

Caracal: terrifying claws...

Cheetah: super speedy...

I'm good at hiding from things on the ground, but that's not the only place I have to keep an eye on...

LOOK UP!

THE EAGLE

No! The hare spotted me! I was so close to a tasty treat. I'm an eagle, and I can soar through the skies to spot my breakfast, lunch, and dinner from above.

NAME:	Eagle
TYPE:	Bird
HOME:	All Over the World
FOOD:	Carnivore
PREDATOR OR PREY?:	Apex Predator

I'm an apex predator in these grasslands, and I'll eat anything! What do I want today?

Mouse: a tiny treat...?

Wildebeest: some lovely leftovers...?

Hare: a hopping feast...?

I'm so tired today—I'm going to SCAVENGE some of the lion's wildebeest leftovers rather than catch my own dinner.

WAIT, WHO'S THAT?

17

THE STRIPED HYENA

That eagle has the right idea! I'm a striped hyena, and I'm a scavenger. Why would you waste time and effort to catch your own dinner when you can just steal someone else's?

NAME:	Striped Hyena
TYPE:	Mammal
HOME:	Africa
FOOD:	OMNIVORE
PREDATOR OR PREY?:	Apex Predator

As I keep to myself, nothing much likes to eat me, so I'm also an apex predator. I'm licking my lips looking at today's menu...

Caracal: the lion's spares...?

Aardvark: the lioness's leavings...?

Topi: the lion's leftovers...?

Wildebeest: the cheetah's scraps...?

TURN THE PAGE... BUT QUIETLY...!

THE CHEETAH

Psst! Be quiet and don't alert my prey. Had you forgotten about me? Good—that's exactly what I wanted. I'm a cheetah, and I hunt silently until I'm ready to pounce. I can see three of my favorite meals, but which should I go for?

NAME:	Cheetah
TYPE:	Mammal
HOME:	Africa
FOOD:	Carnivore
PREDATOR OR PREY?:	Apex Predator

Wildebeest: delicious but big and strong...?

Hare: tasty but not very filling...?

Thomson's gazelle: yummy but hard to catch...?

I'm going for the gazelle. They're very fast, but I'm the fastest land animal in the world—and I do like a challenge...

GRASSLAND FOOD WEB

The arrows follow where the energy goes. Can you follow the energy from the sun all the way to the apex predators?

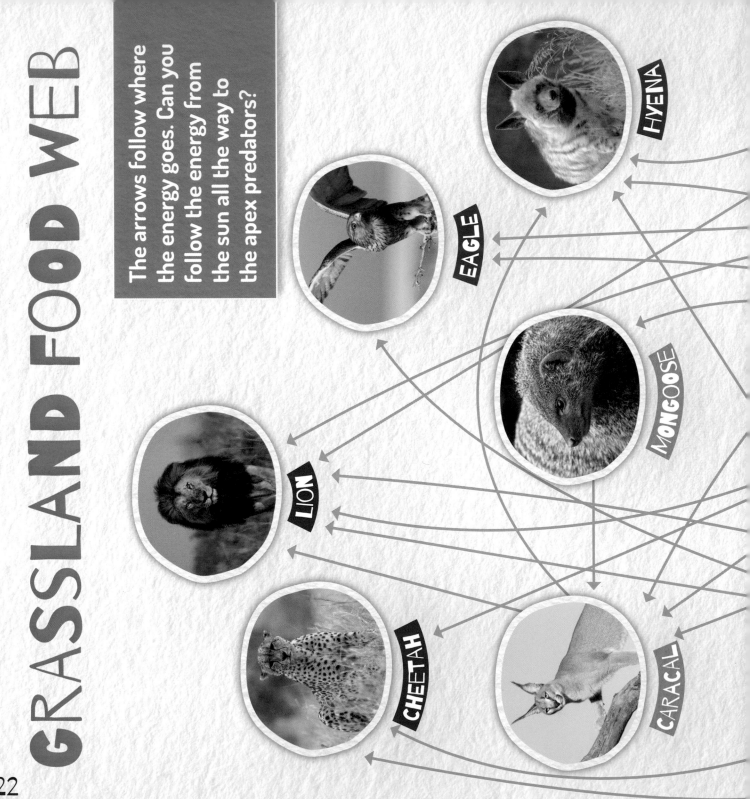

HYENA

EAGLE

MONGOOSE

LION

CHEETAH

CARACAL

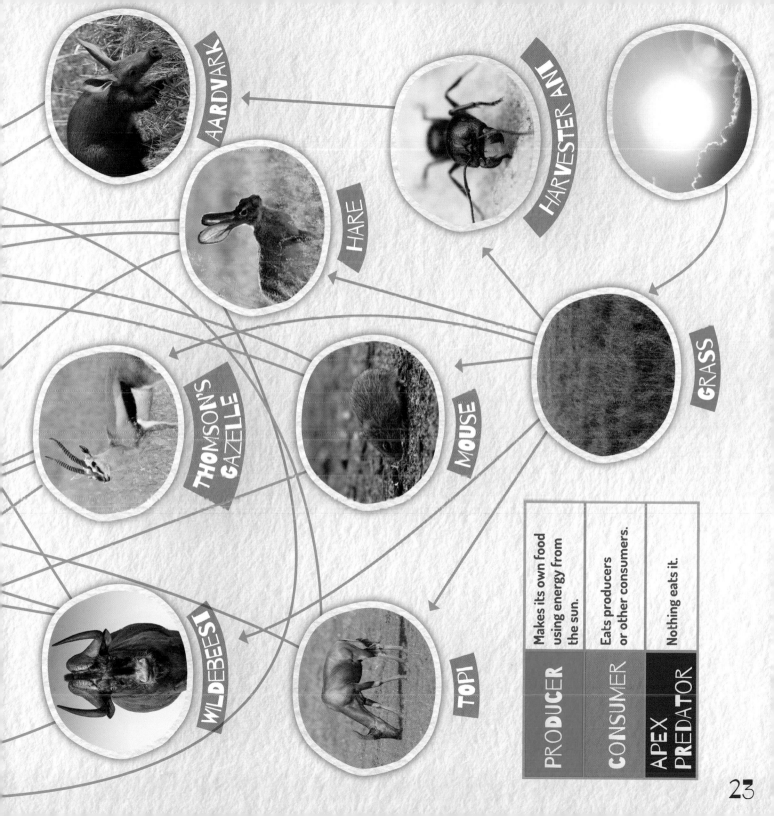

AARDVARK

HARVESTER ANT

HARE

THOMSON'S GAZELLE

MOUSE

GRASS

WILDEBEEST

TOPI

PRODUCER	Makes its own food using energy from the sun.
CONSUMER	Eats producers or other consumers.
APEX PREDATOR	Nothing eats it.

GLOSSARY

apex predator   The top predator in a food chain, with no natural predators of its own.

carnivore   An animal that eats other animals instead of plants.

herbivore   An animal that eats plants instead of other animals.

mammal   An animal that has warm blood, a backbone, and produces milk.

omnivore   An animal that eats both plants and other animals.

predator   An animal that hunts other animals for food.

prey   Animals that are hunted for food.

savanna   A large area of flat land with grass and very few trees.

scavenge   To feed on other animals that are already dead.

INDEX